How The
Best
Get
Better®

Printed in Toronto, Canada. The Strategic Coach Inc., 33 Fraser Avenue, Suite 201, Toronto, Ontario, M6K 3J9. This book was designed and typeset using the Macintosh publishing system by Marilyn Luff. Cover graphic illustrated by Suzanne Noga.

This publication is meant to strengthen your common sense, not to substitute for it. It is also not a substitute for the advice of your doctor, lawyer, accountant, or any of your advisors, personal or professional.

If you would like further information about The Strategic Coach® Program or other Strategic Coach® services and products, please telephone 416.531.7399 or 1.800.387.3206.

Library and Archives Canada Cataloguing in Publication

Sullivan, Dan, 1944-
        How the best get better [kit] : the art and science of
entrepreneurial success / Dan Sullivan.

ISBN 1-896635-29-6

        1. Success in business. 2. Entrepreneurship. I. Title.

HB615.S943 2001   658.8   C2001-903588-8

This book has a companion set of over two hours
of audio recordings that can be downloaded at
strategiccoach.com/go/HTBGB. Either reading
the book or listening to the audio will be of benefit.
However, I encourage you to do both in order to
receive the greatest impact.

Welcome to

How The Best Get Better®

Because they can change the technical frontiers and reshape public desires, entrepreneurs may be even less limited by tastes and technologies than artists and writers, who are widely seen as supremely free. And because entrepreneurs must necessarily work and share credit with others and produce for them, they tend to be less selfish than other creative people, who often exalt happiness and self-expression as their highest goals.

George Gilder
The Spirit of Enterprise*

Table of **Contents**

How The Best Get Better®

Global forces, unleashed by the application of microchip technology, are causing entrepreneurial revolutions everywhere. The changes that have occurred during the past few decades due to the combination of microtechnology and entrepreneurism have been remarkable. However, the changes that have occurred constitute only a beginning: We haven't seen anything yet.

Ahead lies a complete bottom-to-top entrepreneurial transformation of global society. Political, economic, educational, and social structures are being reorganized in fundamental, far-reaching, and non-bureaucratic ways.

Those who are entrepreneurially minded are delighted with this transformation because it allows them to access extraordinary capabilities and opportunities. Many others—whose security and status remain based on bureaucratic systems—are deeply disturbed and threatened. As the patterns of human activity over the next decades may prove, there seem to be three different responses to the growing tide of entrepreneurism in the world:

1. **The best get better:** The most successful entrepreneurs are taking advantage of new capabilities to create greater wealth and autonomy for themselves, while providing new opportunities for millions of others.

2. **The beginners get braver:** Those entrepreneurs at beginning levels of success, and those dissatisfied and open-minded bureaucrats who know they must become entrepreneurial, are gaining confidence and direction from the example of the best entrepreneurs.

3. **The bureaucrats become more resistant:** Those hard-core bureaucrats who cannot imagine any other existence for themselves are doing everything possible to impede entrepreneurism. Even though bureaucratic resistance is still very strong in the world, bureaucratic leaders are no longer seen as role models. The executives of the most powerful bureaucratic organizations—government, corporate, military, religious, trade union, and academic—are no longer accorded respect. As a class, they are universally seen as mired in the past, unresponsive to the present, and blind to the future.

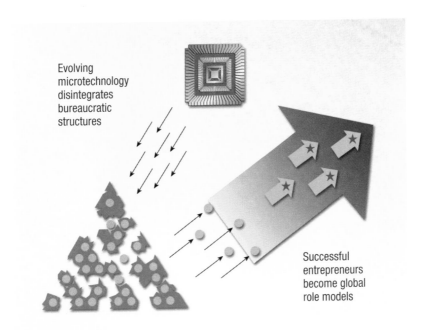

Evolving microtechnology disintegrates bureaucratic structures

Successful entrepreneurs become global role models

Entrepreneurs are global role models and teachers. The best entrepreneurs have learned how to escape, bypass, and transcend bureaucratic structures. They see the past as a resource, they are innovative in the present, and they are visionary with respect to the future. These abilities are necessary to succeed in a world based on evolving technology.

The entrepreneurial example is inspiring and instructive to billions of others who also have a desire to be resourceful, innovative, and visionary. Because entrepreneurs have a non-bureaucratic concept of how the world works, they are able to focus strategically on their most important abilities, relationships, and opportunities with a passionate long-term commitment that is impossible for bureaucratic individuals to match. A global society needs a new global educational approach. The concepts and strategies of the most successful entrepreneurs are the foundation of this new approach.

How The Best Get Better is an evolving lifetime focusing system of concepts and strategies that will enable any entrepreneurially-minded individual to acquire the capabilities—and achieve the results—of the very best entrepreneurs.

The Ceiling of Complexity™

All the growth in a person's life occurs in stages. Within each stage, the individual comes to a point where it is not possible to base further growth upon his or her existing knowledge and skills: The individual has reached a Ceiling of Complexity™. Sometimes this ceiling is permanent, which is why many people fail to grow beyond a particular stage of development.

The problem is experience. Within each stage, we gain experience by solving problems and transacting business. However, this experience has a price—each solved problem, every transaction, adds complexity to our lives. At a certain point, the growth of complexity prevents any further growth of capability, performance, or achievement.

A new state of simplicity is required. No further progress is possible because the existing stage of growth is filled with the complexity of experience—the messes, stuff, details, complications, conflicts, and contradictions that come from doing things a certain way for a long time. One thing immediately becomes clear: Working harder and longer in the existing stage no longer works; in fact, it becomes counterproductive.

A new set of concepts and strategies is needed to achieve a new state of simplicity. It is this new simplicity of thinking, communicating, and performing that enables an individual to break through the ceiling.

All stages of individual growth come from having goals—desiring something new, better, and different. At first, goals liberate and motivate us; once achieved, they hobble and hinder us. Working to achieve a set of goals motivates us to develop specific relationships, structures, and personal habits. Once the goals are achieved, these same relationships, structures, and habits—now firmly entrenched—form The Ceiling of Complexity that prevents the next stage of growth. People become prisoners of their own success, sometimes for the rest of their lives.

A new set of goals is required. New goals—higher and more demanding goals—automatically force us to develop new relationships, structures, and habits. New relationships will provide us with larger opportunities and better results. New organizational structures will provide us with the support necessary to obtain larger opportunities and better results. New personal habits will enable us to obtain higher levels

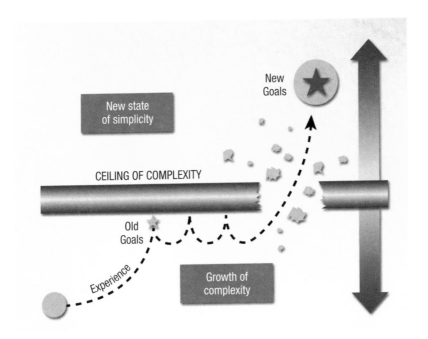

of performance and achievement. All of this means that our current state of complexity must be left behind. When we choose the future over the past, we enter a new stage of individual growth. We break through the ceiling.

The Ceiling of Complexity is a fact of life for everyone, everywhere. Individuals, groups, organizations, industries, and countries all run into The Ceiling of Complexity. Global society is running into ceilings—over-population, starvation, pollution, terrorism. All current stages of growth in all areas of human activity eventually coalesce into new ceilings.

Learning how to break through The Ceiling of Complexity, therefore, is perhaps the most important life skill that any individual can develop.

The first thing necessary to the development of this skill is to change our belief system to accommodate the following concept—The Personal Paradigm Shift.

How The Best Get Better The art and science of entrepreneurial success.

4

The Personal Paradigm Shift

An early definition of the word paradigm is "an example, pattern, or model." This concept was later used in science to refer to a theoretical framework, and was made famous by Thomas Kuhn in *The Structure of Scientific Revolutions*. Subsequently, it has been extended to many different fields and taken to mean "the prevailing view of things." Paradigms are important because, for a while, they make sense of everything, establish relationships between things, and make predictions possible. Paradigms are also applied by individuals: Each individual has a dominant thought pattern about his or her own life—past, present, and future.

Crises cause shifts. Often, in order to overcome crises, new information is required. New information may point to deficiencies in the dominant pattern or model. The paradigm may cease to explain how things work. At first, the new information is resisted and suppressed because it raises questions regarding the individual's investments in the existing paradigm. Human beings hold onto their paradigms until a series of crises forces them to change. Gradually, new information overwhelms the old model, and a new paradigm emerges. The old paradigm is abandoned and adherence to it is now redirected—sometimes suddenly—to this new model. This is called The Personal Paradigm Shift.

Paradigm 1—Rugged Individualism: This paradigm is expressed by the phrase, "I can do it by myself" or "I don't need any support or assistance." It is crucial to the early life development of individualism and self-reliance. But after a while in this rapidly changing world, Rugged Individualism is disabling: It prevents further development of an individual's "Unique Ability." As individuals grow older, those who hold firmly to the Rugged Individualism paradigm are trapped by their weaknesses. This makes it difficult, and then impossible, for them to develop their unique talents and opportunities.

Unless a shift away from Rugged Individualism is made, a person's time and effort are spent on activities where he or she has little ability. The demands of a complex and changing world become greater than the individual's overall comprehension and abilities. Things that once worked no longer do. Knowledge and skills that previously led to success now lead to failure, and the individual's confidence in the future

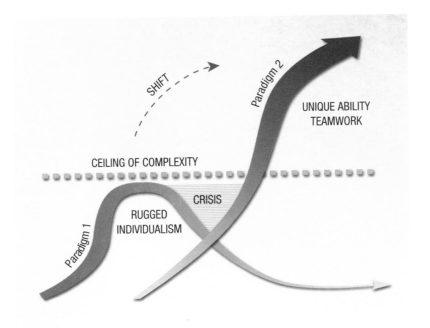

decreases. At the same time, Rugged Individualism prevents the person from recognizing, seeking, and using the abilities of others. Isolation and frustration continually increase.

Paradigm 2—Unique Ability® Teamwork: Rugged Individualism gradually prevents an individual's Unique Ability® from developing into extraordinary performance and achievement. A new paradigm is needed: Unique Ability® Teamwork. Individuals, each with a different Unique Ability, link together so that their weaknesses are transformed by others' strengths.

Instead of being trapped by their weaknesses, individuals in this paradigm are free to focus entirely on their strengths. Unique Ability Teamwork continually expands and adjusts in response to the opportunities of a complex and changing world. Rugged Individualism is left behind.

In order to break through The Ceiling of Complexity caused by Rugged Individualism and make The Personal Paradigm Shift to Unique Ability Teamwork, it is necessary for an individual to have a picture of the future that is not based on who he or she was in the past. This leads to the third concept, The Future-Based Self.

The Future-Based Self

Everyone has three selves: a Past-Based Self, a Future-Based Self, and a Present-Based Self. The Past-Based Self is the person an individual thinks he or she used to be. This self-concept is influenced by powerful memories. The Future-Based Self is the person the individual imagines he or she is going to be. This is influenced by powerful goals. The Present-Based Self is a combination of the other two selves, with either the past self-concept or the future self-concept dominating.

Which concept—Past-Based Self or Future-Based Self—an individual allows to dominate his or her present thoughts, decisions, communications, and actions determines whether he or she will lead a successful, satisfying, and significant life. This decision makes all the difference in the world.

The Past-Based Self resists anything new. A person whose present is dominated by his or her Past-Based Self finds life increasingly difficult, unsatisfying, and threatening. These individuals have difficulty adapting to new situations. This is why they find the present world of global change so frightening. Everything that is important, pleasurable, and meaningful in their lives has already occurred. The future goal of these individuals is to return to patterns of the past. As a result, they are resistant to new knowledge, opportunities, and challenges because anything new and different prevents the desired past from being recreated in their futures.

The Future-Based Self responds to new and bigger challenges. A person whose present is dominated by The Future-Based Self, on the other hand, is attracted to new things. To this individual, it is essential to have a continuous flow of new and bigger challenges. He or she is continually creating, modifying, and improving a powerful Future-Based Self image. What has occurred in the past is not rejected. Those experiences serve as an endless resource that is transformed into building blocks. The purpose of the present is to enjoy constant growth and improvement while laying the foundation for even greater growth and improvement.

Living accidentally or intentionally is a choice. Most people do not consciously create their lives; they react to life, and only retrospec-

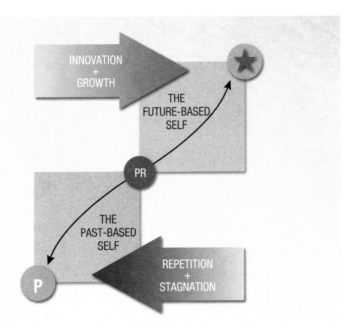

tively differentiate between important and unimportant experiences. People dominated by their Past-Based Selves build the meaning of their lives around things that happen to them by accident. They do not intentionally participate in their lives. Future-based individuals function differently. The Future-Based Self is conscious and intentional. It is continually created over the course of a lifetime through imagination, risk-taking, and focused effort.

The future-based person achieves freedom from the past. Everyone faces his or her own self-generated Ceiling of Complexity. However, people must also break through the Ceiling of Complexity caused by the combined resistance of all the past-based individuals who are operating in society at any given time. No one person can change society. But a future-based person—who is continually creating a more powerful Future-Based Self image—dramatically changes his or her position in society. The future-based person escapes from his or her own past, and then escapes from the control and influence of all past-based individuals.

In creating our Future-Based Self, it is essential to understand how new value and opportunities are created in the world. This is the subject of the next concept, The Two Entrepreneurial Decisions.

How The Best Get Better The art and science of entrepreneurial success.

8

The Two Entrepreneurial Decisions

The French word "entrepreneur" means someone who undertakes a venture—someone who creates something new. Entrepreneurs are always working for their own advantage, but their creative activity invariably benefits many others. The greater the number of entrepreneurially-minded individuals in a society, the greater the advantages and benefits that flow to everyone. There is a direct correlation between the number of entrepreneurs in a country and the standard of living that everyone enjoys. Countries with few entrepreneurs are often more impoverished and backward.

Entrepreneurs distinguish and separate themselves from non-entrepreneurs by making two fundamental decisions. These can be made consciously or unconsciously.

The first decision is to depend entirely on their own abilities for economic security.

The second entrepreneurial decision is to expect opportunity in life only after creating value for others.

These two decisions, taken together, automatically liberate the entrepreneurial individual from political, economic, social, or bureaucratic Ceilings of Complexity that limit and diminish the lives of non-entrepreneurs.

Future-based individuals achieve freedom from dependency. All dependencies, especially bureaucratic dependencies, limit an individual's ability to create a powerful Future-Based Self. With this first decision, the entrepreneurial individual is saying, "No one else has to support me. No one else has to take care of me." Having made this decision, he or she never again has to operate according to the procedures of a bureaucratic organization.

Entrepreneurs achieve freedom from entitlement. The attitude of entitlement says, "I am owed something—by society, by government, by the company, by my family." This attitude imprisons the individual in a lifetime of unfulfilled expectations, grievances, and self-pity. (These results are further described in the next concept.) By making this second decision, the entrepreneur says, "I am not owed anything

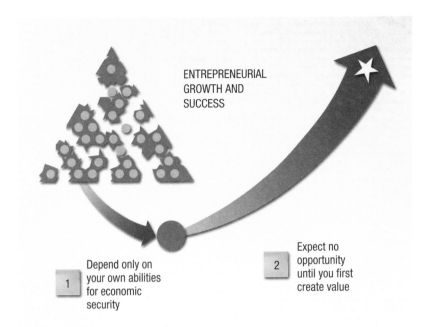

ENTREPRENEURIAL
GROWTH AND
SUCCESS

1 Depend only on your own abilities for economic security

2 Expect no opportunity until you first create value

by anyone. Any opportunity I want must be created by providing something of value to others." As a result of this second decision, the entrepreneur's life becomes a never-ending process of learning, creating, and growing.

Anyone can make the two entrepreneurial decisions. These decisions can be made by anyone, under any circumstances — regardless of age, gender, race, education, status, wealth, or place of origin. The moment the decisions are made, the limitations imposed by dependency and entitlement disappear. New abilities and opportunities become apparent. New decisions and actions become possible. One immediately begins to see life through entrepreneurial eyes.

Bureaucratic dependency is a fundamental Ceiling of Complexity that prevents the growth and progress of most individuals in every society. The next concept, The No-Entitlement Attitude, examines how so many people have become increasingly dependent as their sense of entitlement has grown — and why each individual who wants to grow and prosper must eliminate this attitude.

The No-Entitlement Attitude

The most successful, creative, and happy people in every field of human activity are those who have a No-Entitlement Attitude. This, more than anything else, is what distinguishes the best entrepreneurs from everyone else. Entrepreneurs know right from the beginning that their lives and prospects are in their own hands. They constantly create opportunities for themselves rather than waiting for someone else to do this for them. As a result, the life of an entrepreneur is an endless progression of moving to higher, more rewarding, more satisfying opportunities. While others complain and wait, an entrepreneur creates and moves upward. To appreciate how important—and unusual—this attitude of no-entitlement is, it is necessary to understand the history of the past 70 years.

People experience dissatisfaction in this age of entitlement. Since the end of World War II, Americans and Canadians, especially, have been living in the "age of entitlement." It is interesting to note that during this period of unprecedented progress and prosperity, never have more people been more dissatisfied. The reason for complaint and dissatisfaction lies in the pervasive acceptance of the entitlement belief system in our society.

Society was promised immediate and total perfection. After World War II, particularly in North America, there was extraordinary economic growth for a 25-year period. There was so much wealth and opportunity for bureaucratic expansion that government, corporate, and union leaders began claiming that modern society could be perfected—and in the very near future. It seemed then as if there would always be more than enough money to do and to fix everything. The problems of society— poverty, inequality, crime, disease, unemployment, and so on—would all be solved through government programs and employment in large bureaucracies.

People were promised perfection, and most took the promises seriously. They felt that any obstacles they faced as individuals should now be eliminated, wrongs righted, and deficiencies remedied—by someone else. The major message of the age of entitlement was that individuals were no longer responsible for themselves; a bureaucratic "entitlement society" was now responsible for everyone.

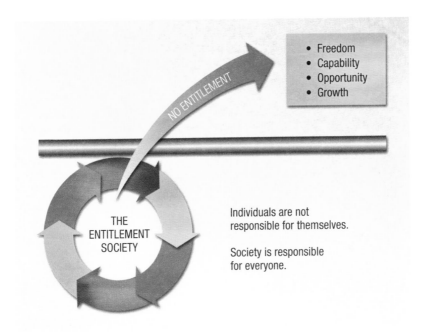

- Freedom
- Capability
- Opportunity
- Growth

NO ENTITLEMENT

THE ENTITLEMENT SOCIETY

Individuals are not responsible for themselves.

Society is responsible for everyone.

But as these foolish and unrealistic promises made by bureaucratic leaders could not be fulfilled, many people felt outraged and cheated. They looked for someone to blame. The period since 1970, with its incessant budget cuts and downsizings, has been shocking and infuriating to those who believe in the entitlement society. Many individuals and groups—regardless of the entrepreneurial prosperity and progress that exists around them—have come to see themselves as permanent victims of society. They are trapped within a closed universe of dependency, disappointment, and grievance.

Everything is created and earned. In order to escape this world of dissatisfaction and complaint—the universe of bureaucratic dependency—it is necessary to have a No-Entitlement Attitude. This means that no one owes a person anything; everything must be created and earned through individual initiative and cooperation. The person with a No-Entitlement Attitude achieves a sense of freedom and capability in a world of unlimited opportunity and growth. Such people are not trapped by unrealistic expectations: They do not expect perfection from the surrounding world. A strong No-Entitlement Attitude permanently enables us to transcend the endless stagnation and unhappiness of the entitlement society.

The Two Economies

Most people think there is a single economy in their society, but, in fact, there are two: The Time-and-Effort Economy and The Results Economy.

The Time-and-Effort Economy, accounting for 80 percent of all people who work, is based on the desire for job security, predictable activity, and guaranteed income.

The Results Economy, consisting of the remaining 20 percent of the working population, is based on the desire for greater opportunity, income, and freedom of action.

These two economies are sharply separated from each other by a "risk barrier" that can only be crossed by making the entrepreneurial decisions outlined in Concept 4. Virtually all individuals start off in The Time-and-Effort Economy and remain there for their entire lives. However, the combination of new technologies and bureaucratic downsizing around the world is causing a growing number of individuals to cross over to The Results Economy. To make this transition from one economy to another requires an individual to give up his or her bureaucratic dependency and attitude of entitlement.

The concept of The Two Economies explains many things that are present in today's world. Most of all, it explains why there is inequality of resources, opportunities, income, and wealth in the world—and why these inequalities are likely to increase during the 21st century. Those who live out their lives in The Time-and-Effort Economy are faced with limited and diminishing prospects, while those who have made the jump to The Results Economy are experiencing expanding capabilities and unlimited opportunities.

People who work in The Time-and-Effort Economy experience loss of control. In The Time-and-Effort Economy, individuals do not create their own economic opportunity; instead, they sell their labor to someone else. In this bargain, they lose control of their working time, abilities, and activities—and they lose control of their future. The billions who belong to The Time-and-Effort Economy deprive themselves of greater opportunities when they sell their labor. Employers tell them what, when, and how to do their work—and how much money they can

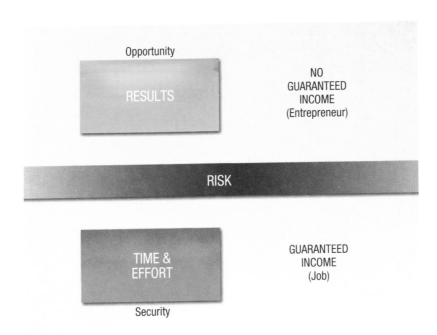

make for doing it. At the same time, employers are constantly striving for greater productivity. This prompts them to seek cheaper labor or automated alternatives. In the worldwide Time-and-Effort Economy, expensive labor is constantly replaced by more cost-effective and productive solutions. Ironically, those whose economic focus is security are most in danger of losing it.

How to create value and opportunity. The Results Economy is different: Instead of focusing on security and guarantees, entrepreneurs focus on creating greater value and opportunity. People who become entrepreneurs give up all notion of guaranteed jobs or incomes. By taking this risk, they actually achieve the possibility of lifetime security—or the opportunity to live by their creativity and capability. Once entrepreneurs prove to themselves that they can make it on their own, they have no need for an employer or a job. What is needed is the opportunity to create value for others. Because entrepreneurs have no guarantees, they must maximize the results of their time and effort: They must seek new methods, markets, and niches. For this reason, they seek change, cause change, and take advantage of change. Those in The Time-and-Effort Economy fear change, while those in The Results Economy thrive on it.

The Entrepreneurial Time System®

Most people live within a bureaucratic time system. They work in The Time-and-Effort Economy, where they organize their lives according to bureaucratic strategies. These strategies, for the most part, require time and effort but do not produce results. They are geared to producing a standardized, competent level of performance, where creativity is suppressed, and extraordinary achievement is discouraged.

As new technologies continually provide new capabilities and opportunities, the first requirement for improving productivity is the replacement of bureaucratic strategies with those based on the successful experience of the best entrepreneurs. The first area of work and life where a fundamental new strategy is needed is time management.

The goal of the bureaucratic time system is to achieve maximum uniformity, repetition, and predictability. This goal is supported by rigid work hours and rigid workdays, and is based on the sale of labor for security: All work hours, days, and weeks are just the same. In tranquil times, the bureaucratic time system leads to boredom. During times of great change, this rigid way of organizing time leads to crises, high levels of stress, and exhaustion—with ever-diminishing results.

The Entrepreneurial Time System® has ever-greater results. It is radically different. It introduces creativity, greater variety, and higher levels of productivity into every aspect of work and personal life. It is implemented by dividing all time into three distinct kinds of days, each of which lasts 24 hours from midnight to midnight:

The Free Day™: The purpose of the Free Day is rejuvenation and enjoyment of physical, mental, psychological, and emotional capabilities. Complete separation and freedom from work-related activities and obligations is required.

The Focus Day™: The purpose of the Focus Day is to maximize concentration of an individual's capabilities on the most important activities, relationships, and opportunities. Complete freedom from non-productive tasks and details is required.

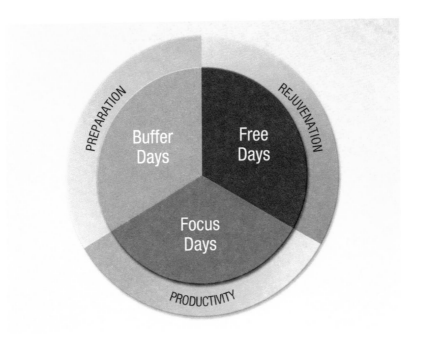

The Buffer Day™: The purpose of this third kind of day is preparation, both for the rejuvenation that will occur during future Free Days™ and the productivity that will occur during future Focus Days™. Complete freedom from the pressures and demands of Focus Day activities and deadlines is required.

The Entrepreneurial Time System results in increased rejuvenation, productivity, and preparation. It provides individuals in The Results Economy with a different time reality. Those who organize their lives according to Free, Focus, and Buffer Days experience a slowing down of time, a sense of having all the time they need to do everything properly and to enjoy everything they do. They also experience the increased confidence that comes from an accelerating cycle of increased rejuvenation, productivity, and preparation.

Free Days lead to increased energy, creativity, and optimism. Focus Days, which concentrate our intelligence and energy, lead to twice the results in half the time. Buffer Days™ lead to increased simplicity and efficiency, and the ability to plan further into the future. Because it continually increases the energy, confidence, and capability of all who use it, The Entrepreneurial Time System is the foundation for the entrepreneurial strategies that follow.

The Largest Cheque®

Individuals hit a Ceiling of Complexity when they become trapped by a certain kind of result. They reach a level of performance and achievement, then progress no further. This is seen in all fields of activity.

Entrepreneurs become trapped by their Largest Cheque®. In the entrepreneurial world, many individuals become trapped by a certain size of "cheque," or the total amount of money received from a client or customer in a single year. Because entrepreneurs unconsciously gear all their efforts to achieving a certain size of cheque, they become accustomed to this result of their performance, and they find further achievement impossible. Everything they think and do becomes rigidly organized around the cheque. Although they want to perform at a higher level, their present result represents the Largest Cheque they can achieve. There are three reasons for this rigidity:

Market relationships: All of the entrepreneur's relationships in the marketplace—clients, customers, centers of influence, suppliers—are geared to a certain size of cheque. These existing relationships are established with individuals who are themselves trapped by their Largest Cheque. The entire network of relationships is static: Everything and everyone within it is fixed at a certain level. Nobody progresses.

Organizational structure: The entrepreneur's existing support structure is not geared toward growth. It is geared toward maintenance of The Largest Cheque. The support team, technology, work processes, and procedures—the capabilities of the organization—are all geared toward getting a certain kind of result and nothing more.

Personal work habits: The entrepreneur is trapped by personal work habits that are geared to the level of the current Largest Cheque. How the individual looks, thinks, talks, performs, and interacts is based on hundreds of little personal habits, and all of these habits are geared to a particular level of performance and result. The habits geared to a $5 million cheque are very different from those geared to a $50,000 cheque; those geared to a $50,000 cheque are different from the habits geared to a $5,000 cheque.

Breaking through the ceiling. To break through the barrier caused by

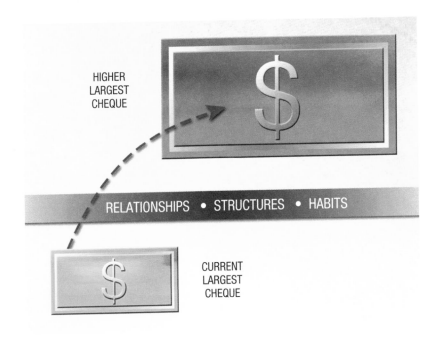

HIGHER LARGEST CHEQUE

RELATIONSHIPS • STRUCTURES • HABITS

CURRENT LARGEST CHEQUE

the existing Largest Cheque, it is necessary to aim for a much larger cheque—in other words, establish a Largest Cheque that calls for a new and more powerful Future-Based Self. The first step is to establish the size of the Current Largest Cheque. This is done by identifying the average amount of the five biggest cheques received over the past 12 months. The new goal is to achieve a much higher average for the five Largest Cheques that will be received over the next 12 months. If the present Largest Cheque is $50,000, for example, the goal for the next 12 months could be $100,000.

Once established, this new Largest Cheque goal immediately impacts relationships, organizational capabilities, and habits. The quality of relationships increases, organizational capabilities are upgraded, and personal productivity habits undergo constant improvement. At the end of each year, the process is repeated, and a higher Largest Cheque becomes the new goal.

Year after year, the entrepreneur's productive time is devoted to relationships that can produce the Largest Cheques, resulting in a constant increase in confidence and opportunity.

The No-Office Solution™

The word bureaucracy comes from the French language and means "rule of the desk or office." Offices, therefore, are where bureaucratic activity takes place, where bureaucratic attitudes are reinforced, where bureaucratic complexity is increased, and where bureaucratic stagnation is the most likely outcome.

In short, offices are generally where non-entrepreneurial activities take place. For most entrepreneurs, the office is the least productive place: It is where they become bogged down in bureaucratic "stuff" and messes. It is where Focus Days become impossible to plan and implement. When entrepreneurs are in their offices, it is very difficult for them to focus on and achieve the next level of Largest Cheque. Offices are where entrepreneurs go to "hide" from their most important activities, relationships, and opportunities. Therefore, offices undermine their purpose, confidence, concentration, performance, and results.

Get rid of the office. The best entrepreneurs in the world have learned to operate without a personal office. They have discovered that without an office, there is no alternative except to focus all their time and attention on productive activities. Without an office, they have discovered that there is little possibility of being surrounded by bureaucratic stuff and messes. And without an office, the best entrepreneurs find that they are increasingly focused on their best abilities, relationships, and opportunities.

Create a superb meeting room. The alternative to an actual office is a superbly designed and decorated meeting room that is always free of notes, papers, files, reports, books, and magazines—all the stuff and messes that undermine entrepreneurial focus. This room should have no work desk and no office furniture, but, instead, a meeting table with a number of comfortable chairs. The decor should be stylish, appealing, and business-like. There should be outlets for phones and computers, but these and other pieces of equipment should be stored somewhere else when the entrepreneur is not using them.

Along with this actual meeting space, there are several rules for conducting daily entrepreneurial business that prevent most forms of bureaucratic sabotage. Everyone on the entrepreneur's support team should understand and adhere to these rules:

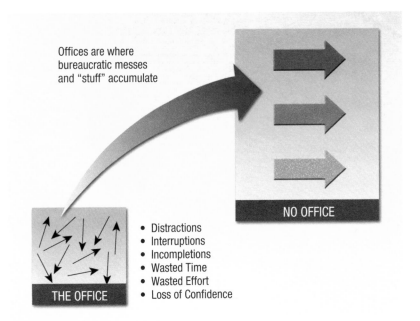

Offices are where bureaucratic messes and "stuff" accumulate

NO OFFICE

THE OFFICE

- Distractions
- Interruptions
- Incompletions
- Wasted Time
- Wasted Effort
- Loss of Confidence

Rule 1: The meeting room must always be free from stuff and messes at the end of each business day.

Rule 2: If the entrepreneur does paperwork in the meeting room, at the end of the day, related materials should be removed and properly filed or stored by a support person.

Rule 3: On a particular day, if the entrepreneur has no one to meet and no paperwork to do, then he or she should not come to the office.

Instead, he or she should be either in the marketplace working on opportunities or taking rejuvenating Free Days. Whether in the meeting room or attending external meetings, the entrepreneur should always be totally focused on developing money-making opportunities. Implementing the decision to get rid of the bureaucratic office will improve any entrepreneur's productivity by 25 percent during the first 12 months. The entrepreneur will subsequently operate entirely within The Results Economy. By combining this No-Office Solution™ with the two previous strategies—The Entrepreneurial Time System and The Largest Cheque—an entrepreneur can double his or her results in a very short period of time.

The R-Factor Question®

The best clients and customers are those with big futures, but how does an entrepreneur determine if this is the case? How can an entrepreneur know whether the prospective client or customer is dominated by a Past-Based Self or a Future-Based Self?

This is a crucial matter. The prospective client or customer may have been extremely successful in the past, yet he or she may lack either the desire or plans for growth and improvement. If an entrepreneur gets into a business relationship with someone who is past-based, then he or she can expect to encounter constant obstacles, roadblocks, complexities, and entanglements. Relationships with a number of past-based individuals and their organizations can seriously threaten an entrepreneur's progress and success.

A past-based client or customer is opposed to growth. Past-based individuals are uncomfortable with the growth of others because growth threatens the power and structures of their Past-Based Selves. Past-based individuals are devoted to activity rather than results, and, consequently, their lives are filled with non-productive activities. Past-based individuals believe they are making progress when they involve an increased number of people in an endlessly complex bureaucratic process.

The following question clarifies whether a person is past-based or future-based in his or her thinking:

> **"If we were meeting three years from today—and you were to look back over those three years to today—what has to have happened during that period, both personally and professionally, for you to feel happy about your progress?"**

This deceptively simple query—The R-Factor Question® (the "R" stands for relationship)—immediately reveals how a person looks at the future. It also determines whether a relationship with that person is desirable.

An individual might not respond to The R-Factor Question. There are only two reasons for this: One, he or she does not want a relationship with you, in which case there is no opportunity; or, two, he or she doesn't have a future vision, in which case opportunity for a useful

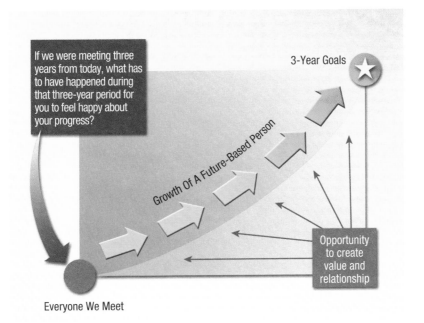

If we were meeting three years from today, what has to have happened during that three-year period for you to feel happy about your progress?

3-Year Goals

Growth Of A Future-Based Person

Opportunity to create value and relationship

Everyone We Meet

relationship does not exist. Either way, you know immediately from the non-answer that the situation is not worth pursuing.

If the person answers The R-Factor Question, an opportunity for a relationship is created. In answering, he or she demonstrates both trust in a potential relationship and a clear desire for a bigger and better future. The answer will always be given in terms of specific goals, objectives, improvements, changes, and solutions. A person's answer to The R-Factor Question clearly defines who his or her Future-Based Self is, and this knowledge enables you to begin creating value in the relationship. Once we know where a person wants to go in life, we can begin assisting his or her progress by contributing our abilities and resources.

The three previous strategies—The Entrepreneurial Time System, The Largest Cheque, and The No-Office Solution—now have a relationship focus. Deal only with individuals who answer The R-Factor Question, individuals who have a Future-Based Self. Future-based clients and customers allow us to be more future-based. They provide us with opportunities for greater performance and results.

The Referability Habits™

The best marketing strategy in the world is to be referable. Being referable means that your existing clients and customers believe in you so strongly that they want to tell others about you. They believe so strongly in you that your success is as important to them as their own. Referability means that your best clients and customers are continually cloning themselves—continually introducing you to those like themselves or better than themselves.

All referability depends upon four habits. Although the best entrepreneurs are involved in diverse kinds of businesses, have very different kinds of clients and customers, and utilize a wide variety of specialized skills and resources, they are all referable for the same reasons. Referability, in all places and at all times, depends upon four crucial habits:

- **Show up on time.**
- **Do what you say.**
- **Finish what you start.**
- **Say please and thank you.**

Although these seem like common sense, a surprising number of people in this world, including entrepreneurs, do not practice these four habits. As a result, these individuals are not referable. They may have brains, talent, charm, and experience, but they continually find that their clients and customers do not refer them. In contrast, those who practice these four habits always get referred into bigger and better opportunities.

Show your clients respect and appreciation. The four Referability Habits are crucial because each of them conveys an attitude of respect and appreciation. They demonstrate respect for other people's schedules, goals, and values. They communicate appreciation because no client or customer will feel taken for granted. Respect and appreciation are permanent safeguards against indifference, overconfidence, arrogance, negligence, and sloppiness—all the reasons entrepreneurs and others lose business and are not referred into larger opportunities.

Brains, talent, and charm are no substitute. Many highly intelligent people are not referable because the main attitude they communicate is

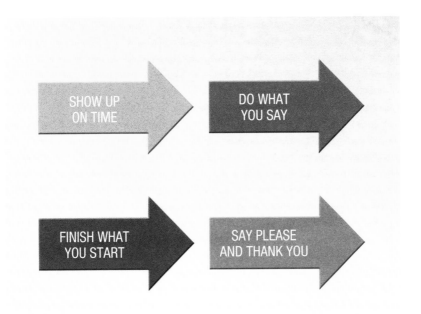

arrogance. Many talented people are not referable because their perfor-mance is erratic. Many charming people are not referable because they are not dependable. Even individuals with specialized skills and years of experience are not referable if they do not demonstrate the respect and appreciation that will prompt clients and customers to talk about them favorably.

Make these habits the basis of your daily philosophy and perfor-mance. Anyone can choose to begin practicing these habits today. The rewards will be immediate: You will be referred to others. Within your organization, make these four habits the basis of all training and procedures. In this way, there will be no breakdowns in service. Nothing will be missed; nothing will fall through the cracks. Everything that your organization does—every communication and every activity—will be perceived as respectful and appreciative by everyone who encounters it. This will result in an endless flood of referrals and unlimited opportu-nities for growth and success.

Delegate Everything Except Genius

All human beings spend their lives in the following zones of activity: Incompetence, Competence, Excellence, and Unique Ability. The success or failure of an individual's life depends upon how much time that person spends in each of these zones. Unsuccessful people spend most of their lives in the zone of Incompetence. Successful individuals spend most of their lives in the zones of Competence and Excellence. And geniuses—those who achieve extraordinary results during their lives—spend almost all of their lives in the zone of Unique Ability.

There are different forms of genius. When most people hear the word genius, they think of IQ, which measures genius in logical reasoning. However, there are many other forms of genius that are not measured by IQ: spatial, musical, kinesthetic, interpersonal, improvisational, and others. In the 21st century, one of the most powerful forms of genius will be entrepreneurial genius—the ability to create value in the form of new products and services. All forms of genius depend upon the total focus of time and attention in an activity zone of Unique Ability. Anyone who identifies his or her zone of Unique Ability, and then spends ten years of concentrated effort within that zone, will begin to think, communicate, and perform in ways that other people see as genius.

Unfortunate childhood lessons must be overcome. Many individuals are never able to identify their zone of Unique Ability, let alone concentrate on it, because they are trapped by childhood training. They learned that the secret to success in life is to work on your weaknesses. Unfortunately, focusing on one's weaknesses usually leads to a preoccupation with mediocre behavior, performance, and results. Focusing on one's weaknesses leads to a constant struggle with oneself throughout life—accompanied by a sense of deficiency, failure, and guilt. In this lifelong pursuit to remedy weaknesses, most individuals completely neglect their inherent areas of Unique Ability. As a result, their lives are filled with a sense of frustration, wasted potential, and missed opportunity.

Focus on uniqueness; delegate everything else. The best entrepreneurs in the world have discovered that the key to success is to focus totally on their Unique Ability and to delegate everything else. Do not work in areas where you exhibit Incompetence, Competence, or even Excellence. Delegate this work to those who have a Unique Ability in

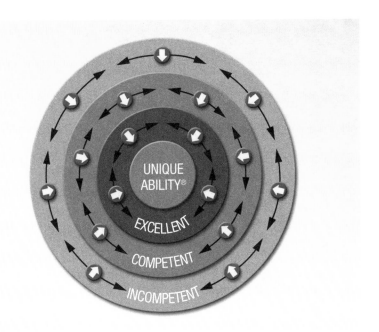

those areas. Unique Ability activities are those that we absolutely love doing, that give us more energy than they consume, and that continue to produce greater levels of skill and better results in relation to the amount of time we invest. When we are in our Unique Ability zone, we experience constant growth, increasing confidence, and an ability to innovate solutions. Additionally, we experience a sense of simplicity, clarity, and serenity, which deepens in relation to the amount of time we spend in the zone.

Unique Ability leads to genius teamwork. Concept 2 described The Personal Paradigm Shift from Rugged Individualism to Unique Ability Teamwork. The main strategy for making this shift lies in focusing on Unique Ability, which both encourages and forces us to delegate every-thing else in our lives to individuals who have strengths where we have weaknesses. In this process, the unique talents of other individuals are brought to the forefront—and those individuals are encouraged to go through the same process of delegation. What gradually develops is not only teamwork, but Unique Ability Teamwork in which each individual is able to spend the major part of his or her lifetime creating value for others using their Unique Ability. Within this Unique Ability Teamwork, all the other concepts and strategies of *How The Best Get Better* are continually integrated, enhanced, and expanded.

How The Best Get Better The art and science of entrepreneurial success.

26

The Road To Economic Adulthood

How The Best Get Better calls for entrepreneurial ways of thinking and acting. In today's mass media and consumer society, there is constant emphasis on individualism. This is misleading. We are told to "do our own thing" or "be our own person," but these and similar messages are given within a framework of bureaucratic values, occupations, structures, and controls. The result is a Rugged Individualism that leads to greater consumption, but not to greater creativity. Rugged Individualism in this bureaucratic sense leads to the further isolation of individuals as workers and consumers, not to personal independence and empowerment.

Escape from the crises of complexity. To achieve real individuality and personal freedom, it is necessary to bypass the traps and snares of bureaucratic Rugged Individualism and embark upon the entrepreneurial road to Unique Ability and Unique Ability Teamwork. The entrepreneurial approach—based on the conceptual and strategic model of the best entrepreneurs in the world—is now the most effective way to escape from the three permanent crises of complexity that envelop those who are still living and working within bureaucratic structures. These are the crises of complexity:

- **Too much happening, not enough time to think and learn**
- **Too little security, not enough opportunity**
- **Too few resources, not enough leverage**

Virtually all the ills of technological society are summed up in these three crises. There can be no bureaucratic solution to the complexity that hinders the growth and development of individuals and their communities because bureaucracy is the cause of that complexity. Greater bureaucracy leads to greater complexity—which leads to still greater crises.

Entrepreneurism represents a breakthrough. Entrepreneurism at the beginning of the 21st century, therefore, represents more than just an individual solution to the crises of complexity. It can also serve as the operating philosophy and methodology for an integrated global culture in which, ultimately, billions of human beings can achieve freedom from bureaucracy, mediocrity, and scarcity.

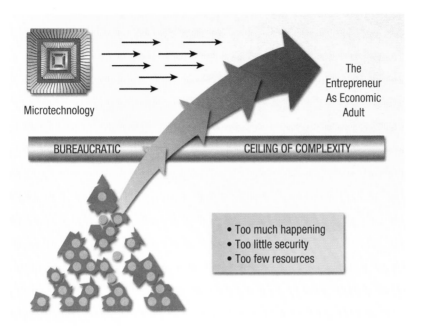

Microtechnology

The Entrepreneur As Economic Adult

BUREAUCRATIC   CEILING OF COMPLEXITY

- Too much happening
- Too little security
- Too few resources

This possibility exists for the first time in history because of the extraordinary capabilities for communication, cooperation, and productivity provided by microchip-based equipment, systems, and networks. These new technologies, developed over the past quarter-century, have been introduced into a world where most organizations still depend upon bureaucratic principles and structures. Consequently, as outmoded structures collapse beneath the demands for faster communication, greater cooperation, and higher productivity, the result has been turmoil, confusion, and increased complexity. Clearly, very little of a bureaucratic nature can be utilized to make the transition to a global economy based on microtechnology. Entrepreneurism on an individual and organizational level is the most promising vehicle.

Economic adulthood. The microchip revolution is enabling individuals to move from economic childhood to economic adulthood—a transition that requires them to be self-directed, self-motivated, and self-managing in a world of continual change. For this transition to happen on a wide or a global scale, individuals must adopt new structures and become more entrepreneurial. The entrepreneurial concepts and strategies of *How The Best Get Better* can serve as the foundation for these structures.

Where The Best Get Better

Understanding the concepts and strategies in this book is the initial step toward a more entrepreneurial life. Much more is required. First, there must be a commitment to a program of activity over a period of years to achieve measurable improvements in all areas of work and personal life. Second, there must be a structure of accountability that keeps one focused on these goals and improvements. And, third, there must be other entrepreneurial concepts and strategies that enable the goals and improvements to be translated into daily actions.

The Strategic Coach® Program. All the concepts and strategies of *How The Best Get Better* come from The Strategic Coach Program, a lifetime focusing structure and process for highly successful entrepreneurs. Participants in the Program have come from a wide variety of industries and businesses, and have succeeded as entrepreneurs; however, they have encountered a Ceiling of Complexity that has blocked their further growth and development.

In spite of their operating as entrepreneurs for many years, these men and women discovered that they were still blocked by bureaucratic attitudes and structures. They had enormous opportunities, but couldn't get to them. Their lives were filled with "stuff" and messes. They spent too much time on non-productive activities, and they experienced enormous tension between their business and personal lives. They felt out of control and off track, and lacked a motivating purpose. Their health suffered, their relationships suffered, and the rewards of being an entrepreneur were hidden by the costs.

In short, all of these entrepreneurs were ready for a fundamental change, for a breakthrough in the way they approached their businesses and their lives. They were ready for The Strategic Coach Program.

The Strategic Coach Program is organized on a workshop basis, offering a full-day session every 90 days. Only experienced and successful entrepreneurs are eligible for the Program: A net income equal to or greater than US/CA$100,000 or UK£100,000—earned over the previous 12-month period—is an entry requirement.

There are four fundamental benefits. Each individual comes into Strategic Coach® for unique reasons and pursues a unique plan of progress. However, on average, within the first three years, participants will derive the following four benefits:

Everyone eliminates all the stuff and messes that interfere with concentration and productivity.

Everyone experiences greatly increased focus on their most important activities, relationships, and opportunities.

Everyone experiences a dramatically increased quality of life— based on a higher quantity and quality of free time.

Everyone develops confidence in their Unique Ability—and in the Unique Ability Teamwork that systematically transforms this Unique Ability into genius.

The successful entrepreneurs who join The Strategic Coach Program usually decide they need a change about a year before they find out about the Program. They decide that things must change; they just need a structure. If The Strategic Coach Program is the structure you've been looking for, please telephone 416.531.7399 or 1.800.387.3206, or, from the UK, call 0800 051 6413. If you would like further information about other Strategic Coach® services and products, please call us at the above numbers or visit our website at *strategiccoach.com*.